EXPLORING THEATER

Lighting and Sound in Theater

George Capaccio

Cavendish
Square

New York

Published in 2017 by Cavendish Square Publishing, LLC
243 5th Avenue, Suite 136, New York, NY 10016

Library of Congress Cataloging-in-Publication Data

Names: Capaccio, George.
Title: Lighting and sound in theater / George Capaccio.
Description: New York : Cavendish Square Publishing, 2017. | Series: Exploring theater |
Includes index.
Identifiers: ISBN 9781502622754 (library bound) | ISBN 9781502622761 (ebook)
Subjects: LCSH: Stage-lighting--Juvenile literature. | Theaters--Sound effects--Juvenile
literature. Classification: LCC PN2091.E4 C36 2017 | DDC 792.02'5--dc23

Editorial Director: David McNamara
Editor: Fletcher Doyle
Copy Editor: Nathan Heidelberger
Associate Art Director: Amy Greenan
Designer: Jessica Nevins
Production Coordinator: Karol Szymczuk
Photo Research: J8 Media

Printed in the United States of America

CONTENTS

Light enhances the appearance of snow falling in this holiday ballet.

CHAPTER ONE
WELCOME TO THE TECH CREW

It is opening night. You've been working on this production forever and can't believe that this is it! In your headset, you hear the stage manager say, "Places everyone ... Go.

House to half ... Go.

House out ... Go.

Curtain up ... Go.

Light **cue** 1 ... Go.

Sound cue 1 ... Go."

You focus your attention on your control board, ready to implement all the lighting or sound cues that you have been rehearsing. You're thinking, "Please let's not have any glitches tonight. No one tripping over my cables. No power outages. No cell phones ringing. Let's all just do this!"

Whether you're working the lights or sound, your contribution to a theatrical production is vital. It involves so much more than making sure the stage is lit and the mics are working. If you enjoy responsibility and working with a team, you'll have two important qualities for these roles. You're someone who likes putting on plays and musicals, but not as an actor onstage, thank you very much.

You'd rather be "backstage," making magic happen. (Actually, "backstage" includes the lighting booth and sound desk—not just what is literally backstage or in the wings.)

Getting Started

If your school puts on performances, it's very likely the tech crew will receive training while the cast is rehearsing. Returning members of the crew will show the new kids how things are done. (Of course, the new kids may have great new ideas!) Your school might also offer theatrical tech as a class or a club.

In some schools, productions have separate tech crews for each area—lighting, sound, set, costumes—with a "chief" for every crew. In other schools, there's one big tech crew; everybody gets involved in helping with every aspect of production.

You may also be able to get involved with your local community children's theater. (It's often called "children's theater" even though it's generally for anyone eighteen or younger.) You'll be meeting kids from other schools as you work together to put on plays and musicals. The after-school or summer workshops they stage in lighting, sound, and safety provide a great foundation for you to serve as a crew member for their productions. Also, check out whether your area colleges are offering technical theater workshops for teens. Searching the internet will let you find not only summer theater camps but also those specializing in tech. Your summer experience could launch a career.

Whether at your school or as part of your

community theater, tech crews welcome volunteers to help out, since there is always so much to be done. They are looking for people who are dependable, are good at following directions, enjoy learning, and have a positive attitude. Enjoying working with electronic equipment is essential; your computer skills are a plus. If you'll be **hanging**—which means installing lights or speakers—you'll learn how to climb ladders safely. (There are tips on ladder safety, along with other smart safety practices, in chapter 4.)

Is This for You?

Theater is a collaborative art form. You're asked to be creative, yes, and to be a problem solver, but you're not entirely free to do whatever you want. Other people may disagree with your ideas. And if they happen to be the director, stage manager, or technical director, you're going to have to "let it go."

For both lighting and sound technicians, a basic requirement is that you enjoy working with equipment. And that involves learning a lot of terminology.

Whether you attend a workshop or learn on the job, you will soon discover that when it comes to lighting, moving a "barn door" lets you control the shape of a light beam, and that when you are "bench focusing," you'll be tuning a lighting **instrument** for maximum light output. And of course, you'll know that maximum light output means making things really bright. **Gel** is something the makeup department may use on an actor's hair, but in lighting, adding a gel will allow you to color a light to affect the mood on the stage.

You'll learn that when you're asked to replace a lamp, you need to get a new lightbulb, and you will know to use gloves since otherwise your fingers would make the lamp explode. You won't look for a key when told to lock the instrument; instead, you'll tighten all the adjustable parts so nothing moves, and it shines on just what it was intended to illuminate. In a tech rehearsal, if the stage manager asks you to "kill the spots," he wants you to turn off the spotlights, possibly to make it more comfortable for the actors.

Be ready to take some notes if you're learning how to run the sound board, or **mixer**. It doesn't make things any easier that many terms have nicknames:

Fader—slider that controls the sound on the mixer

Pot—potentiometer

Bus—main out **channel**

Preamp—preamplifier

EQ—equalizer

When you see your first sound board, the only label you might recognize is MUTE. After a while, you'll understand "that peak light tells us the signal is too loud and is punching the top of our max volume." If you'd like to see a sound board and check whether running one looks like something you'd like to do, see "Sound System Set Up" under video links in the For More Information section at the end of this book.

An important rule for sound is this: Your ears have the final say. You'll be training them to hear

A sound engineer instructs students on how to work this large mixer.

what can be improved and what can be clearer, and how to make it easier for the listener to follow the dialogue or songs.

If you have a background or interest in music composition, here is an area where you can add something truly your own. Access a video-sharing website like YouTube and search for "sound design portfolio" or "sound design demo reel" to hear what sound designers have been creating for theater, film, and games.

Some of the Basics

Theatrical sound and lighting require a combination of technical skill and creative ability. With light and sound, you can:

- Create mood and changes in mood

- Establish the time of day, season, and weather

- Contribute to the sense of reality

- Shift emphasis from one stage area to another (especially with lights)

- Stimulate audience expectations of what is to come

- Build transitions between scenes

- And so much more!

The first on our list—creating mood—is also called creating **ambiance.** Lighting and sound are vital in enhancing the emotions of the story.

Imagine that you are doing a play that takes place in a forest. The scene prep crew has painted some lush trees and bushes that will be used throughout the play. But in act 1, the main character—let's call him Albion—senses something menacing about the forest. (The forest turns out to be the home of a malevolent warlock.) Would you want Albion to be well lit or in shadows? Then, in act 2, he defeats the warlock, and the forest becomes the scene of a raucous celebration. You're working with the same scenery, but now you need to completely change the ambiance. What sort of lighting would you choose?

Music is not just used for musicals. It can do a lot to create ambiance. Think about a castle location. If you're designing the sound for a play based on Bram Stoker's novel *Dracula*, what music would you use? But suppose, in a different play, a castle is the setting for a slapstick comedy. Now what music might you use?

Shifting emphasis is an important role for lighting. With lights, you can draw the audience's attention to what you and the director want them to see. The famous film and theater director Max Reinhardt once said, "The art of lighting the stage consists of putting light where you want it and taking it away from where you don't want it."

Let There Be Light

Most theatrical productions call for a lot more than dimming the house lights—the main lights in the theater—to signal the performance is about to start, and then turning up the stage lights.

The McCandless Method is the name for the basic lighting theory in use today. It was created by "the father of modern lighting design," Stanley McCandless, working in the first half of the twentieth century. He recognized that just lighting the actors from the front makes them look flat and makes it hard for the audience to read their faces—which often reveal their emotional responses to whatever is taking place onstage and/or among the characters. By placing lights to the right and left of

The lighting designer created a special mood for these dancers by using purple and green gels.

the actors, and 45 degrees above the plane of the actors, he was able to sculpt their faces. This made them look more rounded instead of flat.

He then took lighting for the stage an important step further through the use of colors. The primary pair of lights is at different temperatures, one cooler

than the other. One may be blue (cool) and the other amber (warm). This combination gives depth to the actors' faces, much the way stage makeup exaggerates and clarifies facial characteristics and expressions.

Another key advantage of pairing warm and cool lights (called "lanterns" in the theater) is that it conveys the feeling of natural light, which makes the audience sense they are seeing something familiar, real. Shifting the balance of warm and cool lanterns can create the appearance of dawn turning to midday or late afternoon.

Color is adjusted with the use of gels. These are thin pieces of colored, translucent polycarbonate or polyester that are placed in front of the light to filter the light to the desired color. When gels were first used, they were made out of gelatin. Today's filters last a lot longer, though the heat from the light makes them fade over time, so the light crew needs to check them regularly. When gels were still made of gelatin, newbies on lighting crews were told to clean dusty gels by rinsing them in hot water. Imagine their faces when the gels melted!

One of the best things about working with
theatrical lighting and sound is using your
creativity. Sometimes, creativity is born out of
dissatisfaction. It was a dissatisfied actor playing
Peter Pan in 1908 who created a new approach
in lighting design. The actor, Maude Adams, was

This 1905 photograph of
Maude Adams shows her on
stage as Peter Pan.

dissatisfied with the effect of footlights, which lit actors from below, creating unnatural shadows. (Not only unnatural but also spooky!)

The problem she wrestled with was how to counteract the intensity of the footlights. She was searching for something to give the effect of powerful, sun-like light from above and was inspired when she saw a great chandelier in use at the Comédie-Française, the French national theater. Adams proceeded to invent a light bridge above the stage that could hold seven operators who could **focus** and refocus seven spotlights, producing, she claimed, "the equivalent of eight thousand candles."

Teams of operators would be required for decades. In fact, lighting crews were known to wear roller skates, so they could reach all the instruments quickly when they needed to dim each one. It wasn't until 1975 that a computer-assisted memory lighting system was first used at the Shubert Theatre on Broadway in New York. The lighting designer was Tharon Musser; the show was *A Chorus Line*.

If you want to work with theatrical light or sound, you'll be known as a "techie" and serve as part of "the crew." Your fellow techies are easy to spot: They usually wear all black, so the audience will be less likely to see them if or when they need to be onstage to set scenery or props during the performance. The work you'll be doing will be critical to the success of the show, yet it's often a thankless job. After all, nobody goes home whistling the lights. However, without the crew, the actors are just standing on a bare stage in the dark.

The stage manager usually is at the back of the auditorium, giving light and sound cues through the microphone on her headset.

CHAPTER TWO
ALL IN IT TOGETHER

A crisis during a performance of *The Caucasian Chalk Circle* by the Seattle Theater Company illustrates how theater shows require teamwork. The production was very complicated, with hundreds of light and sound cues, and used thirty-six computer-controlled projectors. That's in addition to dozens of costume and set changes. Things were looking good after a great tech week, and the run was off to a lucky start.

Their luck did not last. One night, in the middle of the play, the pregnant stage manager fainted in the control booth. While the wardrobe staff attended to her, the assistant stage manager sprinted from backstage to grab her headset and continue giving cues from the prompt book, the copy of the script with all the cues in it. Although the stage manager was whisked off to the hospital, the show continued without interruption. Neither the audience nor the actors knew that the show had been saved with great teamwork! According to the entertaining and informative book *Technical Theater for Nontechnical People*, mother and baby were fine.

Technical theater includes not only lighting and sound but also scenery, properties, and costuming. You'll all be working together to create an engaging, memorable world in which the actions of the performers take place. If the costumer creates a yellow dress, you'll know not to throw a blue light on it, or the audience will instead see a green dress. Suppose the props master has made a lightweight trunk that will be easy to **strike** (move it on/off the stage). But the director wants it to appear difficult to move. You could provide the sound effect of a heavy box being dragged. By applying your skill and creativity, you'll have come up with a solution that will please both the director and the props master. Best of all, you'll be "strutting your stuff" as a genuine team player.

Teamwork, communication, and respect combine to let everyone enjoy doing their best. There are even competitions for technical people. Each year, the University of Nebraska-Lincoln hosts the International Thespian Festival for high school students and teachers. The Tech Challenge at the festival showcases the different crews competing at their specialty. Search the internet to see what theatrical tech challenges are coming up in your state or region.

Taking Your Cue

The stage manager is responsible for coordinating the cast and crew. He or she works closely with the director to make sure the director's vision is carried out in the actual show. Most plays require both a stage manager and an assistant stage manager. It's the stage manager who will be giving the light and sound cues (and set cues) during the performance, usually from a booth at the back of the auditorium. The assistant stage manager will be managing from backstage. To hear just what that sounds like, see the For More Information section and check out the video link *Stage Manager Calls Cues for "Hairspray."*

A cue means two things. It is the *moment* that you do something, and it is the *something that you do.* This "moment" might be signaled by an action, such as a performer entering the stage, or it might be signaled by a line from the script. (The latter are called "**line cues**.") The "something that you do" could be adding

For this solo, the light operator has used spots with lavender gels, while the sound operator has turned up her mic.

blue light or fading out a sound, like the sound of birds chirping.

Cues are typically numbered—for example, "Light cue 75" or "Sound cue 20." Depending on the preference of the stage manager and the nature of the show, the stage manager may give a thirty-second warning and call "standby" about one or two lines before the cue. Whether you're running the lights or managing the sounds, after you hear the number of your cue, you wait until you hear the stage manager say "Go," which signals the exact moment to take the action. Depending on the practices or conventions of your theater, you may respond with a confirmation such as "75, thank you." Then you'll immediately prepare for the next cue.

Just about any production can make it hard for you to concentrate if you're running the controls for light or sound. You might find yourself laughing at a well-delivered, humorous line, or holding your breath during a dramatic moment. But be careful! You could miss your next cue!

Of course, the actors have just as much responsibility to stay focused. If they improvise a line that they've forgotten, you'll never hear them say the **line cue** that you have listed on your cue sheet. Or if they delay an entrance, you might have lit an area of the stage with no one there. Each team member—cast and crew—has to concentrate on doing his or her particular job.

The word "go" is such an important word in technical theater that most stage managers will not use this word unless they want you to take an action *right now*. Instead, they might explain what they want like this: "For light cue 75, when I say the g-o word, I want you to black out the stage lights for three seconds. Ready? Standby … Light cue 75 … Go." And *then* you'd cut those lights for just three seconds. Blackouts are done occasionally for effect and traditionally at the end of each act. (Lights are commonly blacked out or dimmed after each scene.)

Usually, the stage manager won't tell you *what* the cue is—in this case, blackout. You're only hearing the number of the cue because the stage manager is calling lighting cues as well as cues for sound and for set changes. Your "light (or sound) cue list" has all the specific information about each of your cues. You can see why it's critical that you keep your cue list up to date, so it matches the prompt book. Calling cues well is a skill, so it helps to remember that everyone is learning and getting better with time, including the stage manager.

Working with a script that is brand new? Be sure you and the stage manager are using the same version of the script, with the same page numbers. A lot of confusion can result if the playwright has been modifying the script between performances and possibly changing the pagination. You and the stage manager need to be on the same page, literally!

Teamwork Makes It Work

Here's an example of when teamwork is needed. Say that you, as the lighting director, want a dead black scene shift during a murder mystery. A completely black stage is great for dramatic impact and creating suspense. However, the director needs the **running crew** to make a complicated change in the set. They're

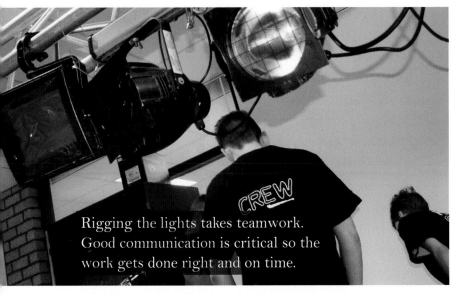

Rigging the lights takes teamwork. Good communication is critical so the work gets done right and on time.

not going to be able to do that either quickly or safely unless you, the director, and the other designers come up with a different plan.

For example, together you might decide that you only dim the lights, but add a strobe effect for dramatic effect, while the sound designer adds some suspenseful music along with the sound of ominous footsteps, maybe those of the murderer. The crew is now able to make the set change safely while the audience holds their breath in anticipation of what comes next.

Keeping the stage manager informed about changes is another example of teamwork in technical theater. Are you planning to place any speakers or other obstructions backstage? Then you need to tell the stage manager. She'll also need to know about any backstage work that will be happening during the performance.

Depending on the size of the technical staff, there may also be a technical director as part of the team.

The technical director may oversee everything tech, including lighting and sound, or may be responsible for overseeing the set and props. It's more common, however, for the stage manager to coordinate the work of all the crews and the actors. For example, which needs to happen first? Hanging the lights or placing the scenery? You won't be able to lower your lights to working height if there's going to be scenery in the way. Teamwork is the name of the game and an important skill you will master as part of a tech crew.

Your Attention Is Vital

During a performance, the audience realizes that the actors and singers need to be on their toes, so they don't forget a line or a lyric. What the audience often fails to realize is that you, as a lighting or sound operator, have just as much at stake. Without your sharp attention, an actor might be speaking in the dark or a singer might be performing with a dead mic. While some may see that as too much pressure, you find it exciting. It's part of what makes the final applause sound so very good.

A professional lighting operator has some great advice for techies: When it comes to the actual show, it's important to remember that it's a performance. You need to stay engaged and fully present. Otherwise, you could miss a cue, only to have an actor walk on stage and start to speak without your having turned on his mic. So you really have to stay involved in the performance.

School, college, and community theater productions typically have rehearsals that last several months. The

This soundboard operator is updating her copy of the script during a technical rehearsal.

lighting and sound designers need to be active from the start. Operators who will run the controls for sound and lighting, plus the **follow spots**, need to be on set for tech rehearsals and for every show.

If you're going to be involved from the first meetings, through set up and tech rehearsals, to the final show, that's a lot of time! Before committing to a production, you'll want to get a specific calendar from the stage manager. After all, you still have to leave time for your schoolwork and other responsibilities and activities. Once a production gets started, it's a real problem to stop and train someone new if they've had to replace you.

Fame Gets a Blackout

There's a funny "lighting blooper" that happened during a professional performance of *Fame*, a musical about high school performing arts students, that illustrates just how important it is for every member of the team to do his or her job—without taking shortcuts. A substitute operator was going to operate a new lighting desk (another name often used for the control board). He got a crash course in using it and felt ready. After all, about 90 percent of the time, the job of the desk operator (also called a Head LX) is to push a large "go" button when the stage manager calls the cues. For example, "Light cue 49 … Go." When the operator pushes the "go" button, the next programmed effect occurs.

OK, so back to our story. Everything was going fine until the operator had to make a small adjustment to a cue because one of the spotlights was a little out of line. This particular cue was for the finale of act 1, when the cast performs the title number, "Fame." The cast strikes a hugely impressive pose, the music comes to a crescendo, a series of spotlights creates a dramatic pattern, and the audience applauds wildly. Normally.

But this time, when he hit the "go" button: blackout! A cast of thirty is onstage singing the end of the big number—the title song—and it's all happening in total darkness! And 1,200 people in the audience are wondering, huh?

What was a very big blooper happened because of a very small mistake. Instead of saving the adjustment by hitting "shift + update," the operator only hit "update." The second mistake he made was that he forgot to test the change. Any programmer would say, "After you save it, *you have to test it.*" This techie learned a valuable lesson about how important his job was for the success of each performance.

Students hang lights following the light plot that was designed for this show.

CHAPTER THREE
THE GAME PLAN

The initial process for the development of both light and sound is the same: read and reread the script. Your aim here is to get a feel for the script and the playwright's style. At this point, you are thinking in general terms and not locking into specific intentions of your own. Staying flexible will help you have a comfortable give-and-take with the director and other designers.

Next, you'll be participating in a design meeting with the creative team. This typically includes the director plus the lighting director, sound director, stage manager, technical director, set designer, props master, and costume designer. Together, you'll be discussing the overall production concept or vision for the production, along with the historical period, location, and other specifics.

For example, the director and designers for *Selfies*—a show that toured high schools—envisioned a very contemporary look and feel for their show. They used music, sound effects, ringtones, and more to create a fast-paced environment that felt contemporary and kept the audience energized.

In a large professional production, the lighting and sound designers are only responsible for the design of their respective specialties; others handle the installation and operation. In school, college, or community theaters, you'll probably be responsible for both planning and execution—or getting the job done—which is definitely a plus, since the more skills you can acquire, the more valuable you will be.

Once the lighting and sound teams understand their role in the overall concept of the play, they can begin to work independently. Let's start with lighting.

Game Plan for Theatrical Lighting

In the video *WICKED: Behind the Emerald Curtain* (listed in For More Information at the end of this book), Kenneth Posner, the lighting designer for

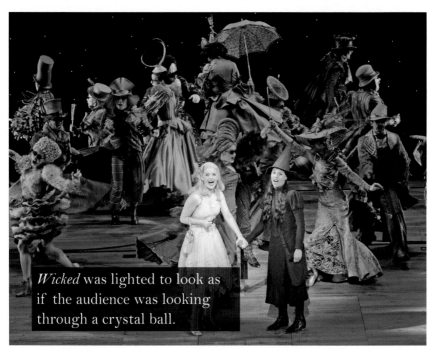

Wicked was lighted to look as if the audience was looking through a crystal ball.

this long-running Broadway show, talks about how he begins designing lighting for a show: "The lighting design for *Wicked* is sort of based on old-school craft and technology and then really, really specifically focused on storytelling—telling the audience exactly where to look. It's about enhancing the audience's experience."

He came up with the idea that the audience would be "viewing this world through a crystal ball, or maybe looking down through a jeweler's display cabinet and seeing these two beautiful gems —these two beautiful characters. After I got these ideas in my head, you distill it down to: How can I achieve these ideas with lighting effects?"

Lighting Basics

As you plan, you'll be thinking about four basic elements in theatrical lighting:

- Intensity: This element refers to how strong (or bright) the light is compared to what is around it.

- Movement: This can have a variety of meanings. For one thing, it means dimming up or dimming down—getting brighter or darker. It also means the motion of a follow spot—the light you use to follow a performer as he or she moves around the stage. Have you ever seen a show where a performer walks or dances *out* of the spotlight? It can be funny for the audience, but not for the spot operator who wasn't paying attention! "Movement" also refers to the pacing of the light cues. Too many light changes can be irritating, while too few can be boring for the audience.

- Distribution: There are different ways to distribute, or shape, light on a stage, using the angle and shape of the light beam. You may be using a soft glow for a gentle scene and later a sharply defined beam to cast dramatic shadows. Spotlights are often round, but you may want to use the shutters to create a rectangular shape to light up a whole actor instead of just his or her face. If you want to create a pattern, like the effect of light coming through the leaves of trees, you can insert a **gobo** into an instrument. A gobo is a metal or glass stencil that, when you place it in front of a lamp, projects the image onto the stage.

- Color: In stagecraft, "color" refers to the color that something on stage *appears to be*—not just the color of the paint or fabric, but also the color of the light. By adding gels to instruments, you can tint the lighting to flatter your actors' faces, cast a warm glow over an entire set, or otherwise add to the impact of a scene.

In addition to lighting, the lighting designer may also be responsible for "atmospherics," which are created with smoke machines and foggers to produce the effect of haze. Haze is valuable when it's important to see the beams of light in the design. Backups (duplicate machines) need to be in place so

During tech week it is critical to test things like the fog.

that if anything breaks down, you're ready to switch systems. One board operator proudly claimed that when stuff fails and he has to use his backups, the audience never notices a thing. And, he added, they don't hear him screaming because he does it (the screaming) in his head.

Lighting Instruments

Along with determining how you want to use lighting, you'll need to know what equipment you have to work with. If the theater has a limited supply of equipment, you might be able to rent additional equipment, provided there are funds to do so. (If renting is an option, then you may have to think about a budget and decide whether there is enough money in the budget to cover the rental costs.)

Theater lights have been called "lanterns" since the days when they burned gas or oil to illuminate the stage. Nowadays, they are more commonly referred to as "instruments." Other synonyms for theater lights are "luminaires," "units," or "fixtures." You will encounter not only many terms but also many synonyms. Every theater group seems to have its own preferred lingo, so in the beginning, you just need to pay extra attention to the words that are used.

There are many different instruments available, but they fall into these basic types:

- An ellipsoidal reflector spotlight has a strong, sharp-edged beam. The name is usually shortened to "ellipsoidal," though the brand name "Leko" is also used. Because of its versatility, this type of instrument is widely used in stage lighting to draw the audience's attention to one person or area of the stage. The beam is shaped with shutters inside the unit, which are controlled by four small adjustors at the sides, top, and bottom. Ellipsoidals can also hold gobos and gels.

- A follow spot is used to follow performers as they move around the stage. Most models will allow you to adjust the beam size, change the color, and lock the beam in place. The light is mounted on a swivel and is run by a "follow spot operator," who stands beside it. With practice, the operator can learn to move the light in sync with the performer, rather than following along behind.

- The fresnel (pronounced fruh-NEL) is similar to the ellipsoidal but gives a softer edge to the light beam, so it can easily blend with other lights on the stage. These are commonly used to light the back of the stage and are positioned overhead to provide a general light. The light is named after the inventor, Augustin-Jean Fresnel, a French engineer who was a French commissioner of lighthouses.

- A PAR can is a nonfocusing spotlight designed for PAR lamps. It's a no-frills, lightweight instrument. (PAR stands for "parabolic aluminized reflector.") Because it's nonfocusing, this type of light is suitable for scenes that need a lot of flat lighting—lighting without a lot of contrast between light and dark, like a bright kitchen in daylight.

- A cyclorama light ("cyc light") is used to illuminate the **cyclorama**, a surface, often a screen, which serves as the backdrop for the entire stage.

- LEDs (also known as "solid state lighting") are new devices that replace conventional lighting instruments and provide color-changing capability. Greater reliance on LEDs seems to be one direction in which theatrical lighting is heading.

- Automated lights (also known as "moving lights" or "intelligent lights") are state-of-the-art lighting tools with incredible flexibility. They contain their own computer processors, which are linked to the lighting control board.

This digital interface means all the properties of the lighting fixtures can be independently programmed and adjusted remotely. A programmer can preset the fixtures to change the focus, adjust the shutters, mix colors, pan, tilt, and even produce strobe effects.

The lighting designer will discuss design ideas and color suggestions with the director and with the rest of the design team. A combination of sketches, collages, photographs, or computer simulations may be used in the presentation. When agreement has been reached (or approval given), it's time to create the all-important **light plot**.

In order to begin the light plot, the set designer will need to provide the ground plan—an overhead view of the stage, drawn to scale, that shows the location of all the items standing on the stage floor. Using the ground plan, the light plot can be drawn, also to scale. This is the diagram used by the tech crew to hang the lights. The light plot specifies:

- What instruments are to be used

- Where each instrument will be located

- What color will be added, if any

- Dimmer information (what intensity of light)

- Circuit information

In lighting design competitions, which are held annually for students around the country, competitors are judged on both the concept and light plot they have created for several scenes from a play or musical. They are asked to justify their design: Why did they choose what they did, and how do their choices serve the show? Typically, students demonstrate their concept using materials such as pictures, gobos (templates), and gel or color swatches.

Getting Hung Up

After the lighting design is approved and the light plot created, it's up to the light crew to get the instruments hung and focused. Hanging the instruments is done using the light plot. While large professional productions have a team of electricians led by a head electrician (or "master electrician"), productions at schools, colleges, or community theaters will often expect the lighting designer to assist or oversee the installation. If the equipment is rented, the electrician who delivers the equipment may also set it up.

Some instruments may be hung on light **battens**, which are pipes that hang horizontally above the stage; often, these pipes can be raised and lowered above the stage. Hanging lights is no small task, as some of the lights weigh as much as 85 pounds (39 kilograms). Instruments may also need to be hung in various positions around the theater. This often involves lifting the lights up on a ladder instead of bringing the pipe down to the floor.

Once the instruments are hung, electrical and control cables need to be run to each position; the "control cables" connect each instrument to a dimmer that varies the brightness of the lights. The dimmers are controlled by the **light board**, typically located in a booth at the back of the theater.

Next, the lights need to be focused. Each light will have an assigned "focus area" on the stage. The final focus should put the "hot spot" of the beam on the main actor's head. To know where to point the light, someone needs to stand on the stage. This is because the light really isn't aimed at the ground but about 5 or 6 feet (1.5 or 1.8 meters) above the ground. You can guess why: because that's where the performer's face will be. During this step, color is added to the light.

Competitions are also held for rigging lights. "Rigging" is another term for hanging. In timed events, individuals or teams will hang fixtures from pipes, secure them, wire them, and focus them.

There's another step to be done before you're ready to work with the cast, and that is to program

During the light check, some units are identified as needing to be repaired or replaced.

the show into the **console**. This is done through a process the lighting team calls "cueing." A cue, in this case, is a desired look for the lights during a specific part of the show. The cue can be made by dimming or brightening, changing color, or moving (depending on what your instruments are capable of doing).

It may take you awhile to develop the ability to write cues without first seeing the lights on stage. Trust that you will learn how to do it. Like any other skill, it is an ability that develops with practice. These cues are then saved to the light board, which has a built-in computer processor. There may be hundreds of these cues! The cues are then played back in a specific order during the show. Cueing will be adjusted throughout the tech rehearsals.

Tech Rehearsals for Lighting

Even before you rehearse with the actors, there is a "light check out" in which every instrument in the show is checked. You'll be confirming that all the lights are the desired shape, brightness, and color, and that none of them have burned out. Some of the lighting equipment may need to be repaired or replaced. (To watch a tech rehearsal for the musical *Billy Elliott*, see the video *Broadway 101: How a Broadway Show "Lights the Lights"* listed in For More Information.)

While you have been working with lighting, the cast has been rehearsing with the director. An important part of this process is **blocking**, which means deciding when and where the actors move around on the stage. It's only after the blocking has been finalized that the cast is ready for a tech rehearsal, allowing you to determine exactly where and how you want to light. The light plot will likely be modified during the rehearsal process. A favorite quote of Tharon Musser (who designed the lighting for *A Chorus Line*) tells us something about her process: "A light plot is not a light plot until it has coffee stains and cigarette burns on it." In other words, your light plot will likely go through quite a few changes before the opening night of the show.

Tech rehearsals are the longest and most demanding for everyone. Your first tech rehearsal might be one that is called a "cue-to-cue." It also does not include the actors. Instead, you'll be going from the line cues that signal a change in the lighting (or sound). This rehearsal might be combined with a general technical cue-to-cue, where sound and set cues are rehearsed along with the lighting cues.

Then there's a stop-and-go tech rehearsal, which does include the actors. During this rehearsal, cast and crew will be running the whole show from beginning to end but stopping to work light and sound cues, as well as costume and set changes. This can be a long rehearsal; it's a good time to practice chilling. One or more dress rehearsals may follow, often with tech. Hopefully, everyone is now ready for either the first preview or for opening night.

If you're working with novice actors, don't be surprised if someone wonders why the lights above them are glowing amber and lavender. Just reassure them that these color gels are the most flattering to skin tones. Actors might also need to learn that if their character flips on a light during a scene, they'll need to leave their hand on the light switch for a few seconds, giving you time to activate the stage lights and thus complete the effect. Just another example of how theater involves teamwork.

During tech rehearsals, the director is likely to give you notes on cues that need to be cut, added, or moved. Get those changes to the stage manager quickly so the prompt book can be updated, and any questions can be asked—and answered.

The final rehearsals may include your training a **light operator** to run the console and probably teaching some volunteers to work the follow spots. If someone is running a follow spot and is daydreaming, he's likely to hear the stage manager bark, "Follow spot!" if the actor or dancer moves, and the spot fails to follow. According to a professional lighting designer and educator, the word "concentrate" is the most important word there is in theater. You cannot let your mind wander. Your goal is make each moment of the play the best that it can be.

It's Called a Follow Spot for a Reason

In addition to adjusting lights and cues, rehearsals are important for the follow spot operator to practice his moves. The follow spot operator will also be wearing a headset to receive cues. The follow spot operator may be operating several follow spots, or there may be several follow spot operators for a larger show.

Running a follow spot is trickier than it looks. It's not just about turning the beam on and off at the right times and pointing it at the right person. Even the

This follow spot operator will need to use all of his or her experience to follow this trapeze performer smoothly.

smallest incorrect movement of the instrument will send the light beam several feet off course and distract the audience from the show. Here are some tips that a smooth follow spot operator will want to know:

- Get comfortable. Position the follow spot at a comfortable height, so you can move the spot smoothly and reach the controls easily.

- Loosen up. If the yoke that is holding the spot is tightened down, loosen it, or the instrument will jerk every time you try to move it. (The yoke is a U-shaped hanger that bolts to each side of the instrument, providing support for easy focusing and adjusting.) Many spots have two bolts, so be sure you've loosened the right one and not the one that keeps the instrument at the right height.

- Shutter on/off. Use the shutter to turn the light on and off, not the power switch. It's usually quieter and more convenient to reach. Additionally, some spots have lamps that take a while to warm up, so you can't just turn on the power when you are ready for light.

- Practice! Want to make an audience laugh out loud? Just activate your spotlight only to see it appear on the ceiling, then swerve around until it finally lands on the actor! The spot should be aimed perfectly before you open the shutter to turn on the light.

- Move *with* your partner. Think of the actor as your partner on stage; you want to dance together. To become a smooth operator, enlist a pal to walk around (maybe dance or run) on the stage, randomly changing directions and speeds. Your challenge is to keep the light on your partner without letting it get ahead of or fall behind her.

- Learn the controls. Let's say you're supposed to reduce your spot to just the lead actor's face, but you accidently make the beam enormous. Oops! To avoid making mistakes like this, figure out what all the controls do. Then practice working them until they're second nature.

For the tech rehearsals as well as the performances, the light crew will be working from different locations: The light board operator works from a booth that may be over the stage (another

The house lights are down but not out during this concert performance.

ladder to climb) or at the back of the house. The follow spot operators will usually be located at the back of the house. The running crew (also called the stage crew) includes any backstage people who will be executing light and sound cues, in addition to handling stage sets and props, helping with quick costume changes, and more.

Showtime: House Lights Down

For performances, the tech crew is the first to arrive and the last to leave. Before the show, you'll be going through a preshow light checklist, which you will be given or have written yourself.

Even professionals with years of experience get nervous before the show starts. If you feel anxious, you can use various relaxation techniques to help you settle down and focus. Some light board operators arrive early to sit at their console and run through everything in their head to be sure they won't forget anything.

When the show is over and the curtain comes down, your job is not quite over. You'll need to do a visual check of everything, either now or before the next show. Lamps and gels may need to be replaced. Instruments may need to be cleaned or repaired. Also, the day after the show, you can expect a show report from the stage manager. It will detail anything that needs to be changed before the next show.

In smaller productions, the same techies may be expected to help with both lighting and sound. So even if lighting is your specialty, you'll want to know the basics of theatrical sound. We turn to that next.

The Game Plan for Theatrical Sound

What's the first thing you do as a sound designer? That's right! You read the script. Several times, in fact. The first thing you'll notice is specific instructions from the playwright about sound. Scripts are written in a particular style; the convention is to capitalize any sounds. It may appear two ways:

The doorbell RINGS.

SFX: Doorbell RINGS.

As you've probably guessed, SFX is shorthand for "sound effects," and the desired effect is in capital letters.

You may be working with or creating sounds digitally, using computers and technical software. (Some programs are available free on the internet.) You may also create sounds naturally, using ordinary objects, specially designed props, or even your own movements.

Designers who create sounds naturally are called **Foley** artists. You'll have plenty of opportunities to be inventive, but there are also some tough sound effects that others have figured out how to do already. One of these is the sound of "walking in snow," which is used in the play *It's a Wonderful Life,* for example. The trick: squeeze a box of cornstarch. (Who knew?) Another challenging sound effect is the sound of breaking glass. (Think: safety hazard and repeat performances.) It turns out you can achieve that effect by dropping a small glass bottle onto a small set of chimes. (Watch the video listed in For More Information called *Foley Artist Explains Sound Effects.*)

At this point, it's helpful to make a list of everything you need the sound system to do. How many people will be speaking? How many would benefit from wireless mics? Do you need to play a CD? Will there be musicians who need to be amplified?

Next, you'll want to know the inventory of available sound equipment. If someone has a list, that's great news. The type, amount, and age of equipment that you will have to work with will vary from one theater to the next. Here is what's considered "essential" in a conventional (wired) sound system:

- Speakers, speaker stands, speaker cables

- **Amplifiers** ("amps"): They take sounds from the mixer and add power to them before sending the sound to the speakers.

- Mixer (also known as a mixing board or just "board"): Discussed below.

- Mics: Performers often wear wireless mics attached to their clothing. There are two types that actors wear: lavaliers ("lavs") worn inside or outside the actors' clothing, and body mics, which are the size of a pencil eraser and are concealed in the actor's hair or taped to their cheek, with a small belt pack tucked into the costume.

- Direct input box: Actors wear one unless they're using a wireless mic.

- Mic stands (for singers, musicians)

- Mic cables

- Monitor speakers: These are backstage speakers connected to a mic hanging over the stage, which lets the actors and backstage crew hear what's happening onstage.

- Instrument cables

- Power cables

This might be a good time to watch *Sound System Set Up* for a Georgia Thespians Tech Challenge if you haven't watched it already; see For More Information for the link.

A key requirement is to know the capabilities of the mixer you'll be using. A mixer has been compared to a freeway interchange. Sound comes in from different sources, gets moved around, then is sent someplace else. You're going to learn how to master that—if you don't already know.

Without getting into the details of the different functions of the mixer, there's one thing to know up front: how many pieces of sound equipment the mixer can handle. Every piece of sound equipment has to be plugged into the mixer, each with its own channel. Mixers are described by how many inputs they have. A "sixteen-channel" mixer can handle sixteen sound sources plugged into it.

Most mixers have similar features and functions, and are organized into channels. Each channel is a vertical line, or strip, of buttons and knobs used to control the sound. So if each channel has six knobs, a sixteen-channel mixer will have ninety-six knobs. With their large size and their masses of knobs, buttons, sliders, and cryptic labels, mixers can seem intimidating to the novice sound techie. But if you're interested in creating sound for theater, it won't be long before you begin to appreciate mixers as really awesome instruments.

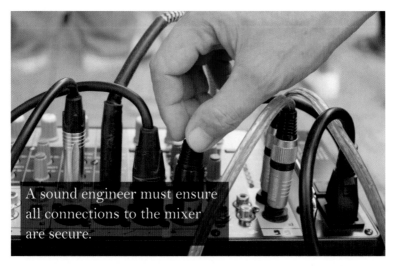

A sound engineer must ensure all connections to the mixer are secure.

From the mixer, the sound is at a low level, not strong enough to create a sound we can really hear. So we're sending the sound out to the amplifiers, one for each speaker. Speaker placement is important because speakers are "directional": they send sound in a particular direction. To prevent **feedback**, avoid putting speakers where they will send sound into mics. If you're getting feedback, test your speakers in different locations.

Let's get back to your production and what it needs. The playwright may have specified sound effects such as "SFX: the BLAST of a train whistle." Other examples:

- Rain, strong wind, thunderstorm

- Clock tolling, a door creaking open

- Heartbeat, glass crashing, tapping sound

- Siren, police radio

A professional sound designer explains, "Sound is a vital element in the show. It often motivates the actor to do the next thing, more so than lighting cues. The doorbell rings. The clock strikes twelve. Sound cues are a big deal; they must be perfectly timed." He goes on to explain that you also need to think about where the sound will be coming from. The sound of the clock striking midnight shouldn't be coming from the same speakers as the preshow music, for example.

As you think further about the script, you may feel the audience's experience would be enhanced with additional sounds. Perhaps a night scene would be scarier with the sound of branches scratching windows.

Ben Burtt: Master at Work

Have you seen the movie *Star Wars*? If so, you might've wondered how they created the hum of the lightsaber, the high-pitched sound of a blaster gun, and the voice of R2-D2, the movie's droid character. Or how about the deep breathing sound of Darth Vader? Where did that come from? All of these sound effects were created by one man—Benjamin "Ben" Burtt Jr., a master sound designer and Foley artist.

Ben Burtt has won four Academy Awards and is known for "voicing" the title character in the 2008 movie *Wall-E*.

Ben began his career making movies but moved quickly into sound, for which he has won four Academy Awards for Best Sound Effects Editing. Before Burtt started working on *Star Wars*, science fiction movies used electronic-sounding effects. He had other ideas. He liked blending in what are called "found sounds." For the Darth Vader effect, Ben breathed into a scuba regulator. The lightsaber hum came from combining the hum of an idling film projector with feedback from a broken television set. That blaster effect? He got it by climbing a radio tower and whacking one of the guide wires with a hammer.

So, while they are called "found sounds," they are usually "found" after somebody goes looking for them. This story says a lot about creativity and a willingness to experiment. Ben is also the originator of a sound effect he calls the "audio black hole." It's that second of pure silence before an explosion to add impact. While his career has been in film, his talents and abilities as a sound designer and Foley artist for movies match those used in theater.

Or a picnic would seem more realistic with the sound of birds chirping. Those are called "sound atmospherics" because they contribute to the atmosphere of the scene.

In addition to sound effects, there's music to consider—before the show begins, between acts, under scenes, and during intermission. You might also program music for the curtain call as well as the post-curtain, when the audience is leaving the auditorium. Under-scene music may be something that you want to compose yourself.

While the actors are concentrating on getting into their specific roles, you will be thinking about the big picture: the whole experience of the audience, from the moment they enter the auditorium until they leave when the show is over. You'll be bringing your ideas to the rest of the design team as you work together to create an engaging production that captures the imagination of your audience. (As with lighting design, your director may welcome collaboration or might expect you to follow her lead.)

Once you have agreement (or approval) for your sound design, you will create a **sound plot** with the following:

- All sound cues and their page numbers in the script

- Precisely when each begins and ends (or how long it lasts)

- How loud or quiet each sound is at each moment

- Any sound effects, and where they are coming from

- Any special effects, such as an echo

- Any music that will be used (including preshow, postshow, etc.)

- What equipment will be used

The sound designer makes a **system layout,** which shows the type and location of speakers on stage, on the set, and in the auditorium. It may also show how all of the sound equipment will be interconnected. The other thing the sound designer creates is a cue sheet, which the sound technicians (operators) will use to run the equipment during performances. The stage manager will also be placing these cues in the prompt book.

Setting Up the Sound

After creating your sound plot and system layout, you'll need to make sure the proper equipment is installed to capture or broadcast the sound. This may well require you to coordinate with the set designer and technical director, especially if you need to "hide" speakers on the stage. (See *Sound on Stage* to hear a sound manager explain techniques she uses; the video is listed in For More Information.)

For example, if your production calls for the actors to listen to an old vinyl record, a speaker installed in "the record player" will create the illusion that the record player is actually working. You'll probably want to install speakers in the proscenium arch to amplify the actors' voices. (The proscenium is the frame around the playing space on the stage.) And there may be additional speakers for the atmospherics,

This technician seems to be asking a soloist to try to sing louder, which is the job of the musical director.

which might be positioned in the wings or suspended above the stage on a batten.

Unlike lighting control boards that each have their own unique set of directions (for that brand and model), there is one software that is commonly used for sound: QLab. It's free for audio playback. The ability to program your sound will make a huge difference in what you're able to achieve. With just one laptop, you can program music to play from the radio onstage and preshow music to play from the main speakers in the theater.

When finishing your setup, you'll be checking that all of the equipment works as intended. Before any of the performers joins the rehearsal, there's testing and fine-tuning any sound effects and prerecorded music. By now, of course, you'll have made backup and archival copies of sound files, cue files, and effects files.

Tech Rehearsals for Sound

At the start of tech rehearsals, a period often called "tech week," you'll be meeting with the director, stage manager, and other production team members for a "paper tech" in which you go through the show cue by cue. Here, if not earlier, mics will be assigned. This needs to be done diplomatically, since actors with fewer lines are not likely to receive a mic and may feel hurt. It's not uncommon for mics to be shared. If you're doing children's theater, be forewarned: some tykes have refused to give up their mic when their role was over and have even taken to hiding in a closet, or other sanctuary, with their mic.

Many theaters can now afford to buy or rent wireless mics. Mics are sensitive instruments, so they need to be placed and handled with care. Lavs should be placed at the top of the performer's chest but not near the throat, since high frequencies can be blocked by the chin and cause the sound to be muffled, or "muddy." If placing a body mic along the hairline, mics and cables can be secured in the hair using clips, combs, bobby pins or elastic headbands. For actors wearing glasses, a mic can be attached to the temple area with a small piece of clear tape. If taping a mic onto the face, never use gaffer tape, as it can cause skin irritation. Instead, use surgical tape, medical adhesive, or clear bandage tape. In some productions, especially musicals, a mic might "sweat out," which means that sweat has stopped it from working properly. Usually, a gentle shaking will start it working again.

If the production is a musical, there will be sound checks for the singers and musicians. To make sure the sound levels are correctly balanced, you may need to mix the different channels together, which can only be done with the singers and musicians. You'll have to "train your ears." Your first priority will be to make sure that whoever is leading *is* leading—that their voice or instrument, if they are playing one, is loud enough and "cutting through the mix." After that, you can worry about letting the other musicians and singers come through.

An important part of these tech rehearsals is practicing working with the sound cues. The stage manager will probably be giving you cues through your headset. Or you may have a "line cue" sheet that links your sound cues to a particular line an actor will be saying. You'll have to be extra alert if your actors are in the (bad) habit of improvising (or making up) their lines!

During these tech rehearsals, the director or stage manager may be giving you changes, so it's important to take notes and fix any cues as needed. Be specific in your note-taking to avoid any complications or misunderstandings. You can't assume someone else is taking notes for you.

Depending on the script, the actors may need to learn how to work with the sound operator. If the actor is turning on a radio, they'll need to leave their hand on it until the sounds fades in. And if they're answering a phone call, they'll have to learn to answer the phone *between* rings. It's just about impossible for you to cut the phone ring exactly as they pick it up. They'll learn this quickly if they answer the phone only to hear it keep on ringing. The next sound they hear will be the audience chuckling.

You'll also want to check your monitoring location. If your monitoring equipment is in a booth with you, it's a good idea to take a walk into the auditorium to hear how things will sound to the audience.

Many community theaters and most professional theaters have a "preview night" before the opening night. This is considered another rehearsal, so you'll want to be prepared to take notes in the production

These technicians perform a check in the theater so they can hear how things will sound to the audience.

meeting that will follow. Then you should be ready for that exciting event cast and crew have been preparing for—opening night.

Preshow Music Up. It's Showtime!

Before each performance, the tech crew will need to arrive early. As the person in charge of sound, you'll need to turn on the sound computer, mixer, amplifiers, backstage monitor amplifier, intercom amplifiers, and any additional equipment. Next, there's running the preshow sound and equipment check.

Both cast and crew can expect to hear the stage manager call "half hour." This is when you are expected to be at your board thirty minutes before the curtain goes up and the show begins. In theater, the calls are not casual, and they are not "around about, maybe, sorta, whenever." The calls are "half hour," "fifteen minutes," "five minutes," and "places."

Just like the light operator, you'll need to be as focused as if you were playing an intense video game. A professional head audio/sound designer once remarked: "It's our job, night after night, eight times a week, six nights a week, to create that perfect image that happened in that one rehearsal when everybody decided *this* is what we're going to try to do every night."

After the audience has left the auditorium, you still have one more job to do: power down everything.

All Together Now: Strike!

A full strike, often called "strike night," is when the entire tech crew comes in to remove everything and return the space to its preshow condition. Sets and props get stored or tossed, hopefully, as intended. Costumes are taken to be cleaned. Lighting and sound instruments are removed and inspected; cleaning and repairing are done as required.

This can be a bittersweet time. Months of hard work are over. No matter how successful the production, you can still have a nasty case of the "postshow blues." Best thing for it: find another show!

Both setting up and striking the set of a production take teamwork.

The lighting crew at this TV studio needs
to use many safety precautions as they work

CHAPTER FOUR

A RISKY BUSINESS

When it comes to theatrical lighting and sound, there's a lot of attention to safety. Why? Well, all that cabling gives you one clue: electricity. Then there are the ladders to climb, since most of the lights and some of the speakers need to be hung. Larger theaters may have a lift, scaffold, or **catwalk**. Safety in the theater requires awareness, common sense, and diligence to eliminate hazards and guard against carelessness.

All theaters are obligated to provide a safe and healthy environment for the actors and crews; if you head up lighting or sound, you'll be responsible for the safety of your crew.

There are recommended practices and safety precautions when working with each of the following:

- Electrical wiring and equipment

- Ladders, lifts, scaffolds, catwalks

- Tools

- Instruments (which get hot)

- Pyrotechnics

- Fog

- Chemicals

- Machinery

Your school or community theater probably has the following basic rules: Submit a parental permission form before you start any technical theater work; learn if there are any tools that you either may not use or may only use if trained, certified, or supervised.

Of Shocking Importance

Let's take a closer look at one of these areas: electrical safety.

Performing arts lighting uses a lot of electricity, so there are risks. Do not ignore even a slight tingle when you feel this sensation while handling a lighting instrument, cord, or component of the equipment. This tingle is an indication that something is wrong; you may be at risk of exposure to a more significant electrical shock. Electrical shock happens when a part of your body completes a circuit between conductors or a grounding source. The effects of electrical shock range from a tingle to death, depending on the amount of current flow and the path of the current through your body.

A basic rule is to be sure that you physically disconnect a fixture before you change the lamp or open the fixture for any reason. That means taking the time to disconnect it *even* if the show is ready to start. There are no shortcuts for safety!

Another important rule applies any time you are focusing or otherwise working with a lighting fixture that is not at zero percent intensity. You'll need to ask someone else to be at the console —or at a remote focus unit—ready to kill the power to the unit in case of emergency. In general, you'll need to know when to have a spotter for stage work.

When you're ready to take on more responsibility, you'll also be making sure that all equipment is properly grounded and that none of the cables,

Lighting technicians need to place ladders close to where the spot needs to be hung so they don't have to reach too far.

circuits, dimmers, or adaptors are overloaded. This includes making sure you don't use lamps with higher wattage than what a fixture is made to handle.

Safety also applies to hanging fixtures onto pipes. Securely attach fixtures with c-clamps and pipe bolts, and add safety cables to each fixture you hang. You can see a great demonstration of this at a theatrical Tech Challenge event, listed as a video in For More Information: *Tech Challenge Event.*

Any follow spot operators need to be thoroughly trained in how to operate this instrument safely. For example, operators should know what to do if the gel in the gel frame begins to smoke. Also, they'll want to wear gloves that can protect their hands from the heat.

While some of these rules apply more to lighting, safe practices for running cables apply to both lighting and sound. Improperly run cables can become a tangled mess that poses trip and fire hazards and hinders troubleshooting to determine why a light or speaker is not working. You'll want to avoid running cables across walkways because they pose a trip hazard, even when taped down. Also, people tromping on cables can damage them, causing short circuits or broken connections.

Be Cool

Fire safety is another big issue that you need to think about. For starters, you'll want to know where the fire extinguishers are kept. Find them before there is a fire onstage! Check that they're not overdue for inspection, and be sure you know how to use them correctly.

Safety gloves should be worn while adjusting the barn doors on a hot spotlight.

The theater probably has a fire curtain as well as flame-retardant curtains. The fire curtain hangs between the stage and the audience. It's there to protect the audience in case a fire should start onstage.

Performing arts lighting equipment also poses fire risks. The fixtures may burn hot, and the lenses used in the lights can magnify the heat. Make sure you use only approved equipment to modify your lights; using unauthorized materials to rig lighting colors or change the shape of the light is a potential fire hazard. Very hot lights should be placed far enough away from anything that could ignite, including paper, plastic, flammable furniture, and draperies. (Remember: flame-retardant does not mean flameproof.)

Watch Your Step

Rigging equipment often means climbing ladders. When rigging, there may be many other students around, working on the scenery or otherwise creating distractions, so it's important to be mindful and follow safety practices. Here are just a few things to help you work safely with ladders:

- Always have someone steadying the ladder while you are working on it.

- Always use both hands to climb the ladder.

- Don't use a ladder that looks damaged or unstable. It may be tempting to use it "just this once," but don't do it.

- All tools carried to the top of a ladder should be tethered to your body using an electrician's belt or straps.

- Never leave anything unsecured on the top of a ladder, even briefly. Imagine what would happen if you were to leave something, even gels or gobos, and someone moves the ladder. The item could fall and really hurt somebody.

- Baggy pants can snag and cause you to fall, so wear clothing that won't get in your way.

The set crew—all those working on creating and moving the sets—also needs to be aware of and practice good safety procedures. For some tasks, personal protective equipment (PPE) will be required. This includes safety glasses, work shoes, hearing protection, respirators, dust masks, arm protection, cotton or leather gloves, hard hats, and bump caps. Your training will likely prepare you to know when to use these types of equipment.

Fancy Footwork Saves the Show

A teenager was part of the stage crew for a touring production of the musical comedy *How to Succeed in Business Without Really Trying*. For this production, the stage crew wore costumes, since they would be moving sets and props on and off stage in half-light.

The cast was working with handheld wireless mics to amplify just their songs; they delivered their speaking parts without amplification. (These handheld mics look like "normal" wired mics but tend to have a bigger body because they include the transmitter and battery pack.)

The mics were to be left on the set for the actors to pick up when they needed to sing. At least, that was how things were supposed to happen.

As you might expect, during one performance, one of the mics was taken offstage during a set change. Realizing the problem before the actors did, this quick-thinking teen grabbed the mic and headed for the revolving door that served as one of the stage entrances. Luckily, this door happened to be close to where the song would be performed.

He spun the door, twirled out onto the stage, handed the mic to the leading man—just as he realized the mic was missing—and carried on, spinning right back into the revolving door to get back offstage.

The audience broke into the biggest applause of the night.

Lesson: Everyone always needs to be "on," not just the actors.

Another area of responsibility is the care of the equipment. Some groups, like community theaters, prefer to rent their lighting and sound equipment since much of it is easily damaged and expensive to replace. You'll earn a lot of appreciation if you do your best to exercise care and caution whenever you handle the equipment or when you train others. If you're working with young children wearing wireless mics, for example, encourage them to take care of their battery packs, so they don't accidentally break the connectors.

Backstage Etiquette

Let's turn from how to keep yourself physically safe to how to protect your relationships. Your connections with all the people involved in the production are affected by how well you practice good theater etiquette. Etiquette—the habits that make it pleasant to be around someone—applies to everyone in theater, from the tech crew to the actors to the audience.

Want to know if the actors and production crew have it together? Watch a tech rehearsal. These rehearsals are often long and exhausting. During tech rehearsals, the tech crew will need time to fine-tune cues and equipment. The most helpful thing actors can do is to pay attention, stay quiet, and be ready to jump from scene to scene. Considerate actors appreciate that the tech crew works crazy hard to make the cast look and sound great.

Theater is a place full of drama. And you know we're not just talking about the script. Emotions run high. Some students are feeling giddy; others are nervous or even scared. This is a great time to think positively. It's also really helpful to avoid gossiping. Everyone has lots of opportunities to make mistakes; talking about them helps no one. Save the drama for the show.

During the rehearsal process or even during performances, it may be tempting to help an actor by giving him or her some tips on how to do a better job. Don't do it. Don't even *think* about doing it. Cast members only want to hear from the director or the stage manager. Although you want to be helpful, it can be confusing if someone gets suggestions from several different people. And the actor might feel you're being rude or questioning his or her acting ability. Besides, your area of expertise is the technical, not the performing aspects of theater.

At the end of a rehearsal, the director gathers everyone and gives notes. Be sure you have something handy for writing your notes. While the notes can be corrections or changes you need to make—and you might really not want to hear them—be upbeat and just say "thank you." It's helpful to remember that everybody gets notes after rehearsals. Even your favorite actor gets notes from the director. If you disagree or don't understand the note, discuss it with the director privately, never in front of the rest of the crew or cast.

For performances, special rules apply:

- Once the house is open, everyone should be backstage or out of sight. This not only applies to the actors in costume but also to the crew.

- Shhhh. If you're working backstage, it's easy to forget how your voice can carry. The only people on the production crew who should be talking are the stage manager and assistant stage manager.

- Put away your cell phone—after you silence it, of course! No texting, tweeting, or taking selfies until after the rehearsal or show. The show deserves all of your attention.

- If you're working backstage, avoid bumping into scenery, backdrops, and the prop table. Not only can your movement be distracting to the audience, but things can break.

- Never move a prop. They are set in specific places, so they can be found in the dim backstage lighting.

Say you were running a spot and your part is over. It's tempting to hang out in the wings to watch the show. Don't, because backstage areas can be tight, and the rest of the crew and the actors need to get around. Also, you don't want to cause a traffic jam as sets are being moved on and off stage.

After a show, you may be collecting mics and other equipment from the actors; they may welcome hearing that they did a great job.

Headset Etiquette

There could be four or more people on headsets during shows: the stage manager, one or more assistant stage managers, the light board operator, the sound board operator, and any follow spot operators. The stage manager may lay down some ground rules regarding what is and is not permissible to say on the headsets. That's because some things can get said that are upsetting to the cast or crew; it's been known to happen. And there's the risk that talking inappropriately over the communication system could "stuff up a cue" (make it inaudible). Credit goes to you if you already know the following "good manners":

- The stage manager rules the headset. Follow his or her lead.

- Make testing your headset a part of your preshow checklist.

A backstage assistant stage manager communicates with the stage manager and operators of lighting and sound.

- Keep your mic off unless speaking (except for the stage manager).

- Keep chatter to a minimum.

- Don't cough, sneeze, or yawn with the mic open.

- When your mic is on, don't move or remove your headset.

- Warn everyone on the channel before plugging or unplugging your headset or belt pack.

- Never discuss anything on the headset you wouldn't discuss in person, center stage, or in front of the audience.

Be Someone You'd Like to Work With

Theater safety and etiquette include many things you should avoid doing. There are also things you can and should do in order to be welcomed into any tech crew and appreciated by both directors and stage managers:

- Arrive earlier than your call, so you are ready to work at the call time.

- You can't say too many words of encouragement or praise.

- Keep things neat and clean, even if it's not your mess.

- Stay focused on the show.

- When you have finished a task, ask what you can do next—don't wait to be told.

- Offer to help others. "Ask not what your stage manager can do for you. Ask what *you* can do for your stage manager."

- Warn others of hazards like hot lights.

- Give others a "heads up" signal when moving overhead rigging.

- When learning something new, aim to learn it so well that you can teach it to the next techie.

- Take great notes after rehearsals and performances.

- Help the actors by not talking with them when they are "in character" as it will break their concentration.

- Watch over the equipment—whether owned or rented—and help others have respect for costly, vital equipment that's often fragile.

- Try to think of things not as "problems" but as "challenges." Put on your positive pants.

Opportunities for audio technicians exist in both live performances and digital production.

CHAPTER FIVE

THE NEXT ACT

If your experience designing lighting or sound for student productions has got you thinking about "next steps," you might consider undergraduate and graduate programs in drama and theater arts. These programs will give you the opportunity to explore the broader field of theater design and technology, or the narrower fields of lighting or sound design.

Making a living in professional theater as a lighting or sound specialist is not impossible. It's also not easy. Professional theatrical lighting and sound designers usually need to have an additional source of income—outside of the theater—to supplement what they earn from working *in* theater. Later in this chapter, we'll explore some of the diverse career paths followed by graduates with a background in theater lighting or sound.

SFX: Opportunity Knocks

If your interest is in sound, you may want to deepen your understanding of audio production and recording. Many people with jobs in this field have an associate's degree, which is obtainable at junior or community colleges as well as technical or vocational schools. These schools introduce students to the major concepts and teach them how to use the various equipment found on the job. If you're aiming higher and want to work in a first-rate recording studio, a film production company, or maybe an animation studio, you'll want to go for a bachelor's or master's degree to boost your credibility.

Course work at a college, university, or technical school will give you hands on experience in audio recording for film and video, as well as for the latest forms of media, like computer animation, video games, computer apps, and internet websites. You can also study the art of creating sounds the way Foley artists do, composing soundtracks, producing multitrack recordings, and recording on location—at an outdoor music concert, for instance.

Here's a sample of career opportunities in the field of audio production:

- Production mixer

- Sound editor

- Game audio designer

- Dialogue editor

- Music editor

- Foley mixer and ADR (automated dialog replacement, or "dubbing")

- Live theater sound designer, engineer, and mixer

- Audio editor for audiobooks

Game designers may need to create new sound effects or music.

Interested in gaming? Your sound experience in theater is a good fit. You can appreciate how well theatrical sound design prepares you for a career in game design when you think about some of the qualities of successful game designers. These qualities include:

- Awareness of audience. Check. You've been thinking about the audience and how you can enhance their experience through sound.

- Efficient. Check. You get things done on time, or ahead of time; you know how to set priorities.

- Creative. Check. After all, wasn't it you who came up with using those great atmospherics from YouTube?

To meet an audio engineer who got a degree in sound design, check out Todd Beyer at Fader King Studios. On his website (see For More Information for the link), you can hear samples of his work as he talks about composing music, reproducing and recording everyday (Foley) sound effects, and doing postproduction audio for movies, TV commercials, and more.

Lighting Your Way

If you've done lighting design for student or community theater, you might decide to pursue a career in this field. As in sound, there is a range of opportunities. For example, lighting designers are responsible for creating the lighting for all sorts of performances, including music concerts (everything from rock to classical), television broadcasts, spectacles like the Olympic Games, musical theater, dance concerts, and even fashion shows and operas.

Another field where lighting plays a key role is architectural lighting. With a background in theater, qualified designers are hired to create the lighting scheme for corporate offices, restaurants, nightclubs, and museum exhibitions, among other types of public spaces. There are colleges and universities around the globe that offer degrees in this field. The International Association of Lighting Designers

(IALD) strongly believes in the "power of light" to enhance human life. The organization awards scholarships and travel stipends to students interested in the architectural lighting design profession.

From Stage to Real World

Even if you are not drawn to a career in lighting or sound, your experience in these areas will help you develop valuable qualities and highly marketable skills, the kind that employers (and colleges) are looking for in applicants. Here's a recent list of the top ten qualities employers value:

1. Communication skills

2. Honesty

3. Technical competency

4. Work ethic

5. Flexibility

6. Determination and persistence

7. Ability to work in harmony with coworkers

8. Willingness to keep learning

9. Problem-solving skills

10. Loyalty

Coming up: a closer look at some of these qualities and their application to careers outside of theater.

A CAREER IN ARCHITECTURAL LIGHTING

Larry French likes to impress upon his lighting design students that "theatrical work is hard and unforgiving." While the work is artistically rewarding, wages for all but the fortunate few are low, and job security is rare. Most designers working in theater have to be constantly on the lookout for the next "gig" to maintain a steady source of income.

Larry's roots are in the theater. His parents worked in amateur theatrical companies, and as a child, he was occasionally allowed to open or close the stage curtains. In high school and college, he acted in plays and musicals, and gradually found himself doing more and more technical work. Eventually, he gave up acting to concentrate on lighting design.

In 1977, his career took off. A major grant opened the door to designing the lighting for theater, dance, and opera companies across the United States. About a decade later, Larry began designing the lighting for the theaters themselves—the buildings in which the shows took place.

This experience inspired him to look beyond the theater for more promising opportunities in television, commercials, film, and architectural lighting, which has become his specialty. As a prominent architectural

Creative lighting adds drama to the nighttime beauty of Niagara Falls.

lighting designer for a leading company, Larry attributes his success to his experience in theater, where he first conceived of the creative possibilities of light in three-dimensional space.

Referring to architectural lighting, Larry French advises his students: "Open your mind and explore an alternate and mostly parallel universe to the theatre. You might be glad you did."

Communication Skills

Good communication skills aren't just about speaking well, and with ease. They also involve the ability to listen well, follow directions, and provide useful feedback. Listening well is something in which techies excel. The stage manager, speaking through your headset, wants to give you directions once—not twice.

Plus, listening well requires the ability to focus and stay present. Every tech rehearsal and every performance has required you to be as focused as a cat watching a mouse or a batter waiting for the pitch. With your headset on and your hands poised at the controls or on a follow spot, you are 100 percent listening for your next cue.

Business journals reporting on the job market agree that the ability to communicate clearly and effectively is one of the most important skills for a young person entering the workforce. Of course, just about every job under the sun requires communication

Like these actors, the tech crew has been developing great communication skills of listening, following directions, and being fully present to the moment.

skills. If you're unsure about how your own skills match up with employment opportunities, it might be time to determine which form of communication you feel most comfortable with.

Oral communication, as its name implies, is about speaking. If you enjoy sharing ideas, having face-to-face conversations (as opposed to tweeting or texting), giving feedback, or maybe explaining how something is done (adjusting sound levels, for example, or replacing gels on an instrument), then the following career options might be worth considering: customer service representative, sales person, public relations manager, or broadcast journalist for TV or radio news. Remember: these are only a small sample of the many occupations in which good oral communication is a must-have skill.

Suppose you're more comfortable in front of a monitor and would rather share your views and opinions via an online blog. If that's the case, then working in social media might be your ticket to a successful future. Companies with an online presence need people to monitor their various social media, like Facebook, Instagram, YouTube, and Twitter feeds. You'll need to keep track of how many "hits" these sites are getting and what users are saying about the company. And you may have to come up with an appropriate response.

If the written word happens to be your strong suit, you could put your writing skills to good use by working as a copywriter for an advertising agency. In that capacity, your job would include writing copy for radio/TV ads, videos, websites, brochures, and other materials to promote a company's services or products. You could also work as a blogger either on your own or for organizations with their own blog.

Work Ethic

Getting to work on time, doing what you are hired to do, meeting targets and deadlines, and working to the best of your ability—that's what it means to have a good work ethic. Doing tech work is a great way to develop your work ethic. Why? For starters, because so much depends on you doing your job to the best of your ability and with an awareness of the needs and demands of your fellow crew members as well as the performers.

You've had to prepare your light or sound plot on time, so the appropriate equipment can be obtained and set up. You arrive at rehearsals not only on time but before the cast does, so you can make sure that everything is going to function according to plan. And you always leave the theater after the actors because you need to stay behind and check your equipment, clean it, and maybe repair anything broken. You've also had to meet your deadline for every performance because the curtain can't go up until you're ready with the lights or sound. When it comes to writing your college admission essay or interviewing for a job, be sure to emphasize all the ways in which you have demonstrated a consistent work ethic.

Working in Harmony with Others

Employers value people who are both likeable and easy to get along with. As part of a tech crew, you've learned that you can work well with all kinds of people, some of whom may be quite different from yourself.

But you're not only working with different personality types; you're also "wearing different hats." In other words, you're performing a variety of roles. As a novice techie, you've had to learn from someone more skilled than you how to do what you do. The reverse is also true: you've possibly trained others in the correct use of the sound or lighting equipment. As an underling, or subordinate, you've had to take direction from the director and the stage manager. As an equal among equals, you've collaborated with your peers in set design and costumes, both making requests and responding to their needs and deadlines. All of these relationships have been opportunities to practice respect, dependability, and hopefully, a sense of humor. Together, these qualities will enable you to perform as a valuable team player.

When asked about what careers his tech students pursue after graduation, one high school teacher of theatrical sound and design answered, "Brain surgery, real estate development—you name it." He went on to explain that members of the tech crew get terrific experience in working as part of a team, which is invaluable in many professions. "When that surgeon is operating, he depends on being handed the right instrument at the exact moment he needs it. He doesn't even need to make eye contact. That's the sort of synchronized work experience they are getting in theatrical tech. These kids learn skills that transcend theater by mega orders of magnitude."

Willingness to Keep Learning

Every new theatrical production brings its own set of challenges, obstacles, and problems. For lighting and sound techies, meeting the challenges, overcoming the obstacles, and solving the problems require a willingness to keep learning and to stay open to new ideas and new ways to do their job. Learning how to "translate" a theater director's vision into creative lighting and sound designs is an integral part of this work.

The willingness to keep learning is one of the core strengths that theater techies possess. They are magnets for information. Any new instrument or control board grabs their attention like a delivery driver showing up at the theater with a stack of fresh pizzas for cast and crew. Since technical theater is a field that is technology-driven, there's a steady supply of new equipment and new apps to learn about.

Problem-Solving Skills

Techies carry a great deal of responsibility on their shoulders. Beyond handling the technical aspects of their job, they use their knowledge and expertise to help the playwright, the director, and the other designers achieve their unique objectives. This is not an easy task. For the tech crew, this involves meticulous attention to every detail of the production and the ability to solve problems as they arise.

Back in the mid-1980s, Kent Dorsey, an up-and-coming lighting designer at the Old Globe Theater in San Diego, California, faced a daunting challenge: create the lighting scheme for a play with twenty-

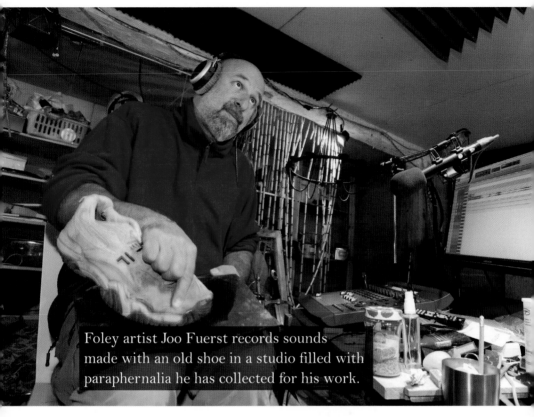

Foley artist Joo Fuerst records sounds made with an old shoe in a studio filled with paraphernalia he has collected for his work.

one different settings, including a Himalayan ice field, a desert, a Cuban nightclub, a jungle, and a swamp—on a small, square stage with various set pieces suspended above the stage. Dorsey eagerly accepted the challenge. To achieve his goal, he aimed and focused 170 lights among the overhead set pieces, along with an array of tiny mirrors and transparent color gels. Crisp blue gels evoked the ice fields; green gels with a dappled shadow pattern suggested the jungle setting. The creative use of sound, combined with Dorsey's lighting and set design, succeeded in turning the Old Globe's small stage into a dazzling panorama of ever-changing environments.

Outside of the theater, companies of all sizes are always looking for people motivated to take on challenges with minimal direction. They appreciate employees who see when something needs to be done and do it. Remember the teen techie who spun onto the stage to hand a mic to a singer in the nick of time? He saw the problem and, without having to be told, did just what needed to be done—with speed and style.

Anyone who has been to a tech rehearsal knows it's a lot about problem solving. If tech were easy, then anybody could do it. But they can't. Duke Ellington (1899–1974), an important jazz composer and bandleader, once remarked, "A problem is a chance for you to do your best." His ability to identify and solve big and small problems is one reason why he was able to keep his large orchestra together for nearly fifty years.

Thanks to your experience in theatrical lighting and sound, you've developed a set of skills that will serve you well in nontheatrical vocations. You've learned the importance of being prepared, dependable, positive, enthusiastic, supportive, self-sufficient, and willing to give 110 percent. Can you think of a job or career where those qualities would not be welcome? Not likely.

GLOSSARY

ambiance The mood or feeling of a scene.

amplifier A device that takes the sound from the mixer and adds power before sending it to the speakers.

battens The pipes that hang horizontally above the stage and on which are hung lighting and sound instruments, plus scenery and curtains. Often, the battens can be raised and lowered, making hanging easier.

catwalk A catwalk is a small bridge above the stage from which technicians can adjust lights, microphones, and scenery.

channel An individual control path on a lighting or sound console that allows the operator to make changes (e.g., dim the lights, lower the sound). The channel can be physical (controlled by a button, switch, or slider) or virtual (controlled by a numeric keypad).

console (short for control console) An electronic apparatus, run by an operator, that converts the settings of various items, such as sliders, switches, buttons, or some form of data input, into a digital or analog signal that is thereby transmitted to a control card, dimmer bank, or some other electronic apparatus. Some control consoles are also equipped with monitors. A control console that has computerized functions and an ability to electronically store data is called a memory board.

cue A command given to technical departments to carry out a particular operation. Typically, the stage manager gives cues. Also, an event that is the signal for a specific action (such as a certain line an actor says).

cyclorama (or "cyc") The drape (or other surface) that serves as the backdrop for the stage, on which light can be projected for special effects. "Cyc" also refers to the lights used to illuminate the cyclorama.

feedback Acoustic feedback is caused by a regeneration of sound leaving a speaker and entering a microphone. This tone—a sustained shriek—is a self-perpetuating cycle which can be stopped by decreasing the volume.

focus Where an instrument is pointed; also, the act of moving an instrument into position so it is illuminating the part of the stage as intended.

Foley Originally, a motion picture term named after Jack Foley, who created sound effects by hand. Today, one can download free Foley sound effects of everyday noises.

follow spot A moveable spotlight that an operator uses to light a performer as they move around the stage; it's also written "followspot." A "follow spot operator" controls it.

gel A thin sheet of colored high-temperature transparent plastic that is placed in a bracket on the front of the lens of a lighting instrument to color the light.

gobo A metal stencil or glass plate that, when you put it in front of a lamp, projects the patterned image onto the stage.

hanging The process of installing lights and speakers; also known as "rigging."

house The term used for the auditorium; the house lights are the main lights that are raised and lowered before and after the show.

instrument A term commonly used to refer to a lighting fixture. Synonyms include luminaire, fixture, and unit. Lamp refers to the lightbulb.

light board Any kind of lighting control, including dimmers and consoles that may be equipped with monitors. A "light operator" runs it.

light plot A diagram that shows what instruments are to be hung and where, including color, intensity, and circuit information.

line cue A line from the script that is a cue for a change such as light or sound.

mixer The sound control desk; it mixes and adjusts levels of sounds from various sources.

running crew The backstage tech crew that makes changes to the set and props, and may make changes for lighting and sound as well as help actors with quick costume changes during a performance.

SFX The abbreviation for sound effects.

sound plot A list of all the sound cues, including when each starts, how long each lasts, how loud or quiet they are, any special effects or sound effects, any music, and the sound equipment used.

strike When the tech crew removes part or all of the set from the stage. It can be done at the end of the scene or act. A "full strike" happens at the end of a run of the show when all the sets plus the temporary lighting instruments and sound equipment are removed.

system layout A diagram that shows the type and location of speakers on stage, on the set, and in the auditorium. It may also show how all of the sound equipment will be interconnected.

FOR MORE INFORMATION

Books

Campbell, Drew. *Technical Theater for Nontechnical People.* 2nd ed. New York: Allworth Press, 2004.

Kaluta, John. *The Perfect Stage Crew: The Compleat Technical Guide for High School, College, and Community Theater.* New York: Allworth Press, 2003.

Lane, Stewart F. *Let's Put on a Show: Theatre Production for Novices.* Portsmouth, NH: Heinemann, 2007.

Stern, Lawrence, and Jill Gold. *Stage Management,* 10th ed. New York: Routledge, 2016.

Videos

Broadway 101: How a Broadway Show "Lights the Lights"
https://www.youtube.com/watch?v=spG3J4ODJSQ
This takes us on a preshow "tech rehearsal" of *Billy Elliot,* the Tony Award–winning musical.

Foley Artist Explains Sound Effects
https://www.youtube.com/watch?v=szyht9jc8PE
Watch an expert demonstrate how he produces sound effects for *It's a Wonderful Life.*

Sound on Stage
https://www.youtube.com/watch?v=GXXbRf_RD6k
Sound manager Yvonne Gilbert explains some of the techniques used to integrate sound effects into the stage and bring the set of a production to life.

Sound System Set Up
https://www.youtube.com/watch?v=TKr-H0te8jc
This is a demonstration of a sound system setup for the Georgia Thespians Tech Challenge.

Stage Manager Calls Cues for *Hairspray*
https://www.youtube.com/watch?v=5TXBqdDAXgE
Listen in as stage manager Mark Stevens calls lighting, follow spot, and set cues for the San Diego REP's musical production of *Hairspray.*

Tech Challenge Event Demonstration: Hang and Focus a Light
https://www.youtube.com/watch?v=O6e1BKLOs4w
Competing teens hang an ETC Source 4 Ellipsoidal and focus the light to a specific shape—all in five minutes, and safely.

Tech Challenge, Thespian Festival 2010
https://www.youtube.com/watch?v=ljMEKB-VUI0
Follow teams as they compete in different aspects of tech: lighting, costuming, blocking, set building, and knot tying.

Todd C. Beyer, Sound Design Profile
https://vimeo.com/117415458
Todd explains his job as a sound design engineer, with examples from commercials and movies, and why he is passionate about his career.

***Wicked*: Behind the Emerald Curtain: Lighting Plot**
https://www.youtube.com/
watch?v=QUKDU3r6MYY
Get a behind-the-scenes look at what can be done with a Broadway musical with big imaginations and a big budget.

Websites

Educational Theatre Association
https://www.schooltheatre.org
The EdTA has more than 3,900 affiliated high schools and middle schools. Their website announces events, provides resources, and more.

Stage Lighting for Students
http://www.stagelightingprimer.com
This terrific website covers the principles of lighting design, lighting technology, an extensive glossary, and more.

Theatre on a Shoestring
http://upstagereview.org
This organization provides how-to articles on sound and set design, as well as helpful links. The Sound Design link will connect you to free sound effects and more.

INDEX

Page numbers in **boldface** are illustrations. Entries in boldface are glossary terms.

ABOUT THE AUTHOR

George Capaccio is an actor as well as a professional writer. His introduction to acting in theater came about as a result of his wife's work in a community theater production. When a fellow actor dropped out of the cast, she asked George if he would step into the role. He did—at the age of twenty-eight. It was his first acting experience and, for George, the beginning of a new career in theater.